TOTTENHAM HOTSPUR

A RANDOM HISTORY

An exclusive edition for

for all your gift books and gift stationery

This edition first published in Great Britain in 2023 by Allsorted Ltd, Watford, Herts, UK WD19 4BG

The facts and statistics in this book are correct up to the end of the 2022/23 season. The data comes from publicly available sources and is presented as correct as far as our knowledge allows. The opinions in this book are personal and individual and are not affiliated to the football club in any way. Any views or opinions represented in this book are personal and belong solely to the book author and do not represent those of people, institutions or organisations that the football club or publisher may or may not be associated with in professional or personal capacity, unless explicitly stated. Any views or opinions are not intended to malign any religious, ethnic group, club, organisation, company or individual.

© Susanna Geoghegan Gift Publishing
Author: Magnus Allan
Cover design: Milestone Creative
Contents design: Bag of Badgers Ltd
Illustrations: Ludovic Sallé

ISBN: 978-1-915902-05-4

Printed in China

★ CONTENTS ★

"THE CREST ON THE FRONT OF THE SHIRT WILL ALWAYS BE BIGGER THAN ANY NAME ON THE BACK,"

said FA and UEFA Cup winner Graham Roberts, who made 209 appearances for Spurs and helped the team to glory in the early 1980s.

★ INTRODUCTION: ★

THE NONSENSE OF
'ALWAYS THE BRIDESMAID'

It's a cliché to suggest that Tottenham Hotspur are 'always the bridesmaid, never the bride'. A cliché and an untruth.

If the average wedding has four bridesmaids, then being always the bridesmaid would suggest that you were, on average, at least in the top five in the great annual nuptial ceremony that is the Premier League. In the 30 years of the Premier League, Tottenham's average position is seventh. In terms of rough, non-scientific estimates, this makes Tottenham always the jovial cousin Simon, never the bride.

The truth of the matter is that Tottenham have only come second once (in 2016/17) in the three decades since the inception of the Premier League, and the team has only started to make a regular appearance in the top five over the last decade. Behind these dry statistics, though, are a handful of important facts.

Firstly, over the last decade, Tottenham's average league position has indeed improved steadily, and they now sit at fifth on average. This makes them literally as good as Arsenal over the last 10 years.

Secondly, Tottenham have consistently been a team that people would rather not face. Sure, there are times when Highbury has been a terrifying place to go, when Old Trafford has been a fortress and the Etihad has witnessed some mythical football, but for consistency and solid all-round family entertainment that doesn't feel like there's a risk you are tarnishing your soul by going there, White Hart Lane and its successor, the Tottenham Hotspur Stadium (no sponsorship, not crass) (at the time of writing), has always been the place to go.

Thirdly, Tottenham have achieved something that very few other clubs have managed: they have become one of the most followed clubs in the world while staying true to their roots and maintaining a reputation for having a very strong presence in their local community. This is not to say that other clubs don't have a strong presence in their local communities, but Tottenham tends to be seen as a nice place. It may not be true that they are always the bridesmaid, but they are the club that you'd be most happy to bring home to meet the family (unless the family in question is from another part of north London. Or west London. Or east or south, to be fair).

★ HARRY HOTSPUR ★

Sir Henry Percy, eldest son of the 1st Earl of Northumberland, was a bold knight in days of yore. He was always ready to attack, and the speed and commitment that he showed in his offensive endeavours earned him the nickname 'Henry Hotspur'. That and the fact that he was always keen to spur his comrades and his horses on with rousing speeches rather than the physical spurs on the heels of his riding boots. Probably. It was the 14th century. Best not think about it too much.

The hot-headed Sir Henry liked nothing more than picking fights with his neighbours. And because of his Northumberland connections, his neighbours, so far as he was concerned, were the Scots and the French.

Now, it could be suggested that as his father was the Earl of Northumberland, he might be justified in harbouring a grievance against the Scots, especially given that, at the time, the border reivers were busily rampaging, pillaging, nicking sheep and generally disrespecting the authority of landowners all over the north of England. The French, though, were many miles to the south and so, while they were presumably meddling in affairs of state all over the British Isles, it could be suggested that it's a bit of a stretch to call them neighbours of Sir Henry in his family's northern seat.

It has long been true that the egos of the English aristocracy are greater even than the lands that they hold, but bold Sir Henry also owned extensive lands in the south of England. This probably, in his head, gave him the right to pick fights with the French on neighbourly grounds. That and the cash that the king offered in return for his support.

Among the lands that Hotspur owned was a stretch of land in north London called 'Tottenham Marshes', and 500 odd years later, in around 1882, a group of plucky lads were looking for a name for their recently formed association football club. They decided to call the team 'Hotspur Utd', which was two years later updated to 'Tottenham Hotspur Football Club', to honour both their neighbourhood and their long-fallen feudal lord.

It is possible that they came to this name after calling in marketing experts who formed several consulting sub-committees, huddled around whiteboards drinking lattes and discussing their suggestions with panels of independent advisors. It is more likely that they were just a bunch of likely lads having a natter around a streetlamp on Tottenham High Road one evening just before the dawn of the 20th century.

Now, we could have got through this whole section in 50 words, because really it boils down to some kids in north London 150 years ago deciding to name their team after some bloke that owned the land 500 years before that, but the history of the club is almost as important as the sport that it plays.

"EVEN NOW, WHEN I GO OVER TO MY MOTHER'S HOUSE AND DIG OUT THE OLD TRACKSUIT TOPS I WORE, IT MAKES THE HAIR STAND UP ON THE BACK OF MY NECK. I LIKE TO THINK I AM PART OF A SPECIAL FAMILY"

Steve Perryman sums it up nicely.

PREMIER LEAGUE: A GAME OF TWO ★ HALVES ★

Tottenham's Premier League position over the last three decades has been very much a game of two halves. Between 1992/93 and 2007/08, the Spurs enjoyed an average league position of 10th. While they were in with a sniff in both 2005/06 (see page 155) and 2006/07, the team did not qualify for the UEFA Champions League at any point. After 2008/09, the team, on average, has taken fifth position and qualified for the UEFA Champions League 50% of the time.

Is it witchcraft that has driven the change? Not really. It's a combination of factors, including: a long-term commitment to the youth team, which has led to the emergence of some truly world-class talent; an ambitious – and, mostly, understanding – chairman; and, most recently, the creation of one of the world's best stadiums for football.

So, rather than witchcraft, it's alchemy – the bringing together of a variety of elements that has driven Spurs to the brink of success over the last few years.

Having Harry Kane and Heung-Min Son on the team hasn't hurt much either.

TOTTENHAM IS THE ONLY TEAM TO HAVE WON THE FA CUP WHILE OUTSIDE OF THE FOOTBALL LEAGUE. THEY WON THE TROPHY IN 1901, BUT DIDN'T JOIN THE LEAGUE UNTIL 1908/09.

•TOTTENHAM HOTSPUR •

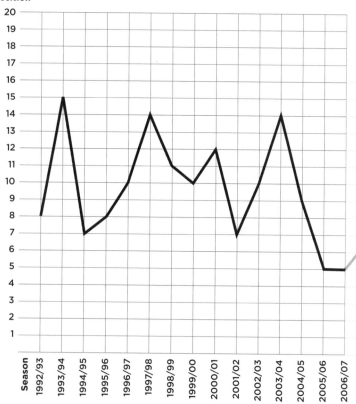

PREMIER LEAGUE
★ FINAL POSITIONS ★

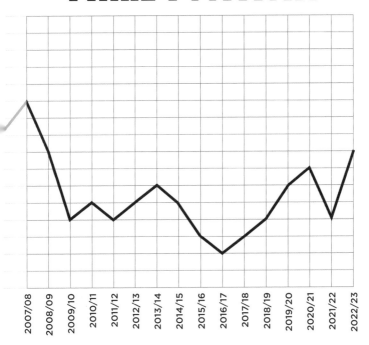

2007/08
2008/09
2009/10
2010/11
2011/12
2012/13
2013/14
2014/15
2015/16
2016/17
2017/18
2018/19
2019/20
2020/21
2021/22
2022/23

★ WALTER TULL ★

History can be challenging, but it's important to face it head on. Walter Tull was an exciting inside forward who signed for Tottenham in 1909 at the age of 21, becoming only the second mixed-race professional football player in England. He appeared to be living up to his promise, taking part in the 1909 tour to South America and scoring twice in 10 appearances during the early weeks of the 1909/10 campaign.

Unfortunately, he suffered significant racial abuse from the opposition fans, with one contemporary newspaper suggesting that he was confronted with language that was worse than that you would expect to hear at Billingsgate Market. He lost his place in the first team and signed for Northampton Town shortly afterwards.

Tull joined the army at the outbreak of World War I, fought at the Battle of the Somme and on the Italian front, and became the first mixed-race officer to lead soldiers on the front line of the conflict. He was killed in action in northern France in March 1918, while leading an attack on the Western front at the Somme. He was recommended for a Military Cross for bravery.

TOTTENHAM MARSHES AND NORTHUMBERLAND ★ PARK ★

When Tottenham was formed, the team played its football on the Tottenham marshes, but because this was public land, spectators could not legally be charged for watching a match. Thousands of people saw the delights of a Tottenham game for free, but the Tottenham of the 1890s was struggling to make ends meet and raise the three guineas and tuppence that they needed to be competitive in the Victorian transfer window (which didn't exist, but you get the point).

And so the team moved to a pitch on Northumberland Park, which they rented for the princely sum of £17 per annum. By comparison, a two-bedroom rental flat on the same street was recently available for £1,350 per calendar month – although there was a sign on the listing saying, 'No Ball Games Allowed', so that might explain the price difference.

Either way, the first stand, which could hold 100 people, was built at Northumberland Park for the 1894/95 season, but as word spread about the majesty of the football regularly on display there, the team quickly began to outgrow its new home. In 1898, 14,000 people are said to have attended their match against south Londoners Woolwich Arsenal, with many more stuck outside. Some fans, in an attempt to get a better view of the action on the pitch, climbed on top of a refreshment stand in the ground. It collapsed, and dozens were injured.

Spurs needed to march to a new home.

STILL MORE NONSENSE OF 'ALWAYS ★ THE BRIDESMAID' ★

The other way to look at the 'always the bridesmaid, never the bride' cliché that is often levelled at Tottenham is to look at the number of times the team has enjoyed runner-up medals in the FA Cup, the oldest domestic football competition in the world™.

Chelsea and Manchester United have all been second best eight times. Liverpool and Arsenal have been nearly men seven times. Manchester City also ran five times.

Tottenham? Only once. That's as many times as the legendary Clapham Rovers or the mighty Notts County. Even the Old Etonians (it was the 1880s, things were different then) have come second four times, and you know how much they like trying to take control of everything (and how often they make a mess of it).

TOTTENHAM'S LARGEST WIN
WAS A 13-2 VICTORY AGAINST
CREWE ALEXANDRA IN THE
FA CUP IN 1960, WHILE THEIR
LARGEST LEAGUE VICTORY WAS
A 9-0 DRUBBING OF BRISTOL
ROVERS DURING TOTTENHAM'S
BRIEF VISIT TO DIVISION TWO
IN 1977/78.

THE OPPOSITION: ★ ARSENAL ★

As a London-based club, Tottenham have many local derbies, but the real spice is saved for close neighbours Arsenal. The rivalry between them has been central to the story of both clubs for well over a century, kindled when the team, formerly known as Woolwich Arsenal, made the move from south to north of the river (that's the river Thames for non-London folk), encroaching on what had been Tottenham's traditional stomping ground.

Weirdly, when Arsenal formed in 1886 (originally as Dial Square Football Club, then Royal Arsenal, then Woolwich Arsenal), Woolwich was officially part of Kent, and wasn't incorporated into London until three years later. Part of the reason for the move was that Woolwich, at the time, was relatively sparsely populated, so they needed to move to north London – where there were more people – to ensure that they could attract players.

Whatever the excuse, Tottenham was well established in north London by 1913 when their formerly south London-based rivals showed up in their borrowed Nottingham Forest kits.

The tension between the two clubs started to get really tasty six years later when Arsenal took what should have been Tottenham's spot when the First Division was expanded from 20 to 22 teams. It has never been proved, but rumours of grubby deals persisted around the ballot that decided which team would be promoted.

Having two such prominent teams in proximity was always going to create the potential for friction, but it should be pointed out that Spurs let Arsenal use White Hart Lane's facilities during World War II. At the time, Highbury was being used as an Air Raid Precaution (ARP) centre and bomb shelter, so the two sides haven't always been at loggerheads.

To give you a sense of the rivalry between the two clubs, though, it is worth noting that in the men's game, 45 players have moved from one side of Merseyside to the other, 39 have played for the red and the blue sides of Manchester, but only 15 have moved across the three miles of north London that separate Tottenham and Arsenal. There are some thresholds that people are very wary about crossing.

The two teams have been playing competitive football matches against each other since 1896, but looking at the years of the Premier League/Premiership up to the 2021/22 season, the pair had met 62 times, with Tottenham winning 26% of the time, drawing 37% of the time, and doing the other thing for the balance.

Interestingly, though, if you look at Tottenham's home record against Arsenal, they win 45%, draw 39% and lose only 16% of the time. Obviously, the away statistics are less pretty, although the proportion of draws are relatively consistent. Which is nice.

Without getting too far into crunching the numbers, it is worth pointing out that of the 62 times the two clubs have met in the Premier League, there have only been five 0-0 draws, the last of which was in 2009. So you are almost guaranteed entertainment when north London clashes.

LES FERDINAND GRABBED THE 10,000TH PREMIER LEAGUE GOAL IN TOTTENHAM'S 4-0 DEMOLITION OF FULHAM IN DECEMBER 2001, KNOCKING A SWEET CROSS INTO THE BACK OF THE NET AFTER 20 MINUTES.

★ BILL NICHOLSON ★

Bill Nicholson had an association with Tottenham Hotspur Football Club that lasted more than half a century. He joined the club in 1936, initially as a ground-staff boy on £2 per week, making his first team debut against Blackburn Rovers in 1938. His career was impacted by the outbreak of World War II, but he returned to the club in 1946 and spent eight years on the pitch.

He was a key part of the 'push and run' strategy that Arthur Rowe developed and used to devastating effect as he managed the team to their successful pursuit of the 1950/51 league title, the first time that any team had won the title in the year that they were promoted from the Second Division. 'Push and run' is now known as the 'one-two' and is a staple of the game, but the way that Spurs implemented it was a revolution for the sport; it went on to influence sporting philosophies, such as the Netherland's 'Total Football' system, decades later.

Nicholson scored with his first touch after 19 seconds on his international debut, but only played for his country once, preferring to focus his efforts on staying fit for Tottenham. As he pointed out – with a certain amount of Yorkshire bluntness – it was Tottenham that paid his wages after all. The legendary Billy Wright's presence on the

England team may also have played a role in keeping him out of contention.

He took his management badges as his playing career came to a close, rising through the Tottenham ranks to become first team coach in 1955 and then manager in 1958. His time in charge started well, with a 10–4 drubbing of Everton, and he led the team to the first double of the 20th century in 1960/61, winning both the League and the FA Cup.

He remained in charge until 1974 after delivering a string of trophies. While his relationship with the chairman in the mid-1970s was strained – and he spent some of the period working for other clubs – by the end of the decade he was back where he belonged. He remained involved with Tottenham as honorary president beyond his retirement at the start of the 1990s.

★ ST HOTSPUR DAY ★
I

In the year of our Lord 1991, on the 14th day of April, the proud men of Tottenham did face their most arch-rivals, Arsenal, in what historians shall forever call the semi-final of ye Football Association Cup.

Proud Gascoigne of Geordieland did make the first impression after a mere five minutes, fair belting a free kick into the top right to vex Arsenal's David Seaman and send him and his threadbare moustache tumbling to the floor as the onion bag did billow behind him.

Lineker, well-regarded son of Leicester, added to Arsenal's lamentations, poaching a second after 10 minutes with the traditional tip of his outstretched toe. Flummoxed defenders in red did fall on him 'by accident' but their crashing presence could not dim his smile.

Alan Smith, his shorts indecently tight even by the fashions of the day, did find one in reply, using part of his head and all of his luck, to beat Erik Thorstvedt, the noble protector of the Spurs goal, as the first half came to a close.

But the day was sealed for Tottenham, when Lineker danced past the leaden Tony Adams in the Arsenal defence, beating sad Seaman to find the back of the net once more. Terry Venables, himself an FA Cup winner with Spurs in 1966/67 (against Chelsea no less), smiled benignly from the dugout.

In honour of that day each year, 14th April has become St Hotspur Day, a national holiday celebrated up and down the British Isles and even across the world (or at least certain parts of north London).

TOTTENHAM GOALKEEPER
ERIK THORSTVEDT BECAME
THE FIRST PREMIER LEAGUE
SUBSTITUTE WHEN HE
REPLACED IAN WALKER IN
THE LEAGUE'S FIRST SEASON
IN 1992.

"ANY PLAYER COMING TO SPURS, WHETHER HE'S A BIG SIGNING OR JUST A GROUND STAFF BOY, MUST BE DEDICATED TO THE GAME AND TO THE CLUB. HE MUST BE PREPARED TO WORK AT HIS GAME. HE MUST NEVER BE SATISFIED WITH HIS LAST PERFORMANCE, AND HE MUST HATE LOSING."

Bill Nicholson OBE makes an early bid for immortality in the inspirational quotes scene on social media.

"I HAVE ALWAYS HAD THE DEEPEST RESPECT FOR BILL NICHOLSON AS A PERSON AND AS A MANAGER. THE SPURS BOSS IS AN HONEST YORKSHIREMAN, AND YOU WILL GO A LONG WAY BEFORE FINDING A STRAIGHTER CHARACTER THAN THAT. BILL HAS NEVER WAVERED IN HIS DETERMINATION TO GIVE WHITE HART LANE FANS THE BEST."

Legendary Liverpool manager
Bill Shankly.

33

★ TED DITCHBURN ★

Ted Ditchburn joined Tottenham in 1937 as a member of the White Hart Lane ground staff, only signing on as a professional footballer shortly before the outbreak of World War II in 1939. Once the conflict was over, though, he became a stalwart of the Spurs team as it developed the 'push and run' strategy that ultimately led to them becoming the 1960/61 double-winning side.

Ditchburn's large hands, inherited from his father who was a professional boxer, gave him a natural advantage when trying to catch the ball, and he struck up a good understanding with right-back Alf Ramsey, nicknamed 'the General', who later managed England to World Cup success in 1966. They began to move beyond route one football, where the goalie or defender launches long balls up the field in the direction of the attacking players, preferring short, precise throws to build attacks from the back.

He enjoyed an unbroken 247 matches for Spurs between 1948 and 1954, helping the team to promotion as Second Division champions in 1949/50 and First Division champions in 1950/51 along the way.

He played for England six times, and was in the 1950 World Cup squad, although he did not play. Many agree that he would have played more for his country if England had not had such a long list of strong goalkeepers in the immediate post-war period, although some also suggest that nerves did him no favours when he pulled on the 'three lions' shirt.

Either way, he was a very talented man who played 418 times for Tottenham before an injured finger forced him to step back from top-flight football in 1958. He continued to relish the sport, however, spending six years as Romford's player-manager between 1959 and 1965.

AUDERE EST FACERE: ★ TO DARE IS TO DO ★

Tottenham's motto, *audere est facere*, translates from Latin to 'To dare is to do'– a strong statement about the power of dreams. It's a similar sentiment to 'Aim for the moon, and even if you miss, you'll find yourself among the stars.' But you would struggle to fit that on a badge unless you used a very small font.

As an aspiration, 'to dare is to do' is a great phrase, and the use of Latin gives it a veneer of class. If it was being created today, it would probably be something like the more staccato 'Dare. Do.', but let's face it, marketing is a fickle thing, and fashions rise and fall like waves. The nice thing about having a heritage slogan is that you can move it in and out of the foreground as fashions dictate and as you choose, without having to go through the difficult process of introducing a whole new slogan and hoping that fans pick it up.

It also has the flexibility to adapt to circumstances. Tottenham responded to the Covid-19 pandemic in several ways, such as increasing its support for fans and the local community; offering the stadium as a drive-through testing site; delivering food for those in need; providing online fitness training to help keep people active; and sending personal messages to keep people's spirits up.

Doing the right thing and supporting the community is not marketing, but marketing does play a role in getting the message out that support is available. The fact that the organisation could tie it all together under the phrase 'To dare. To do. Together' underlined that priorities had to change, even if only for a little while.

'To dare is to do' is a slogan that's easy to understand, it has heritage, flexibility and is recognised by people all over the world. Cynics might argue that it's marketing fluff, but it's good marketing fluff.

"TOTTENHAM HAVE IMPRESSED ME. THEY HAVEN'T THROWN IN THE TOWEL EVEN THOUGH THEY HAVE BEEN UNDER THE GUN."

Bobby Charlton, England hero and occasional pundit, puts the English language through the wringer.

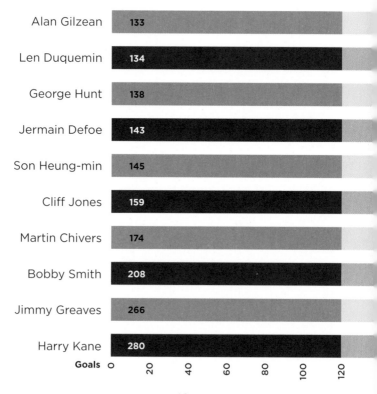

Player	Goals
Alan Gilzean	133
Len Duquemin	134
George Hunt	138
Jermain Defoe	143
Son Heung-min	145
Cliff Jones	159
Martin Chivers	174
Bobby Smith	208
Jimmy Greaves	266
Harry Kane	280

Goals 0 20 40 60 80 100 120

TOTTENHAM'S LEADING ALL-TIME ★ GOAL SCORERS ★

(ALL COMPETITIONS)

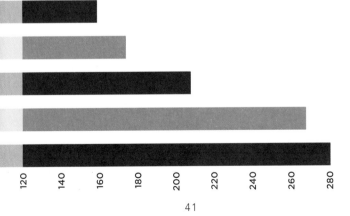

120 140 160 180 200 220 240 260 280

DANNY
★ BLANCHFLOWER ★

Danny Blanchflower captained Tottenham in the double-winning year of 1960/61, when they won the League by eight points and beat Leicester in the FA Cup final. This feat made Tottenham the first team of the 20th century to win the double (Aston Villa had previously achieved it in 1896/97).

A defensive midfielder with an exceptionally precise cross, Blanchflower made 337 league and 382 overall appearances for Tottenham, and received the Football Writers' Association's Footballer of the Year award in both 1958 and 1961 (an award most recently won by Gareth Bale as a Spurs player in 2012/13). The team also won the FA Cup in 1962, which enabled them to go on and lift the European Cup Winners' Cup in 1963.

Blanchflower, by all accounts, rarely changed his mind once he'd taken a position. Back in the day, there was a television programme called *This Is Your Life*, which involved surprising a celebrity or sportsperson with what was called the 'Big Red Book', which was said to contain the story of their life, and then getting them to come to a studio or theatre that was filled with family, friends, comrades and colleagues from various stages of their life and career. They would share a range of sometimes fascinating and occasionally hilarious anecdotes, live, in a primetime slot on national TV.

Blanchflower's career included stints in the RAF around the world alongside his footballing exploits, and as a footballer-turned-journalist he was fairly comfortable in front of the camera, so he was expected to be an excellent subject for the programme.

The lights were on. The cameras ready. The entire Spurs team, Blanchflower's wife and dozens of other people he knew were waiting, the nation was settled expectantly in front of the telly ... and he took one look at the presenter, realised what was going on and scarpered. No amount of talking to him would convince him to take part.

★ WHITE HART LANE ★

White Hart Lane was one of the most famous stadiums in the world. It was built on a nursery site owned by one of London's largest brewers, and setting it up involved demolishing an array of greenhouses and physically moving the stands from Northumberland Park to the edges of the new pitch.

Tottenham moved to 'the Lane' in order to increase club revenue, a move that paid off in a big way. Club records show that the gate receipts from the first official match held at the new ground – a 4–1 demolition of Notts County at the start of September 1899 – were a whopping £115 18s. 3d. Still, it's better than they'd been getting before.

Why it came to be called 'White Hart Lane' is, unfortunately, shrouded by the mists of history, which is a slightly over-dramatic way of saying that no one really knows because no one thought to keep tabs on all the information as the club went through its formative years.

45

It could be that it was named after the nearby White Hart Lane railway station or a lane leading to the stadium that also went past a pub called the White Hart.

Either way, Spurs bought the freehold for the new site, as well as some additional adjoining land in 1905, which enabled expansion and allowed the club to admit around 40,000 people on match days. Expansion and redevelopment meant that capacity is thought to have reached around 80,000 by the early 1930s.

In its heyday in the 1950s, the Lane is known to have regularly hosted around 75,000 Tottenham fans (and a smattering of visitors who were welcome so long as they wiped their feet and remembered their Ps and Qs), but by the advent of the 21st century, grown-up considerations such as safety, meant that the numbers were restricted to around 36,000. There's no doubt that 36,000 people can make a whole lot of noise on a Saturday afternoon when the game's going well, but in a world where Tottenham need to find the money to sign £50 million players on a regular basis in the second Elizabethan age, 36,000 wasn't bringing enough money through the turnstiles.

Like Northumberland Park in the 1890s, the team needed a modern stadium with higher capacity that would help bring in the revenue. As a result, Tottenham decided to move to a new stadium that would match the team's ambitions. And so, in 2017, after 118 years and 2,533 (mostly) competitive Spurs matches, White Hart Lane was demolished, and the Tottenham Hotspur Stadium rose majestically in its place.

SPURS WERE THE FIRST TEAM TO LIFT THE UEFA CUP, WHICH WAS ESTABLISHED IN 1971.

★ JIMMY GREAVES ★

Jimmy Greaves came through the Chelsea youth system in the late 1950s, scored 124 First Division goals in over four seasons, including a goal against Tottenham Hotspur on his first team debut. In 1961, he moved to AC Milan for eight months or so and then finally started his career properly by joining Tottenham at the end of the year.

He is said to have signed for Spurs for £99,999 to avoid being under the pressure of being known as the first £100,000 player – because rounding-up numbers wasn't invented for another quarter of a century. It clearly worked because he scored a hat-trick on his debut at White Hart Lane.

During his nine years at White Hart Lane, he made 321 appearances and walloped in 266 goals, won the FA Cup twice, the Charity Shield twice, and the European Cup Winners' Cup. Until the 2022/23 season, he held the record for the most goals scored in the English top flight with 357, of which 266 were scored while wearing the white of Tottenham. After six decades, his record has finally been beaten by Harry Kane, who scored his 267th goal for Spurs in the 1-0 defeat of Manchester City in February 2023.

In his spare time, he helped England to win the FIFA World Cup in 1966, although an injury in the group stages meant that he was kept out of the final by Geoff Hurst and, as a result, didn't receive a winner's medal until the rules changed in 2009. He also helped England come third in the 1968 UEFA European Football Championship.

After retiring, Greaves formed a successful broadcasting partnership with former Liverpool player Ian St John, presenting seven series of *Saint and Greavsie*, a light-hearted football discussion show that showed his humour, warmth and extensive knowledge of the game. Greavsie sadly died in September 2021 aged 81. Coincidentally, Spurs and were playing Chelsea in the next game (the two teams for which he played most of his career) and so a minute of applause was held to commemorate him.

"THE BIGGEST REGRET OF MY WHOLE FOOTBALL CAREER WAS LEAVING WHITE HART LANE IN 1970 … MY INTEREST IN FOOTBALL WEAKENED AFTER THAT. I WAS HEARTBROKEN."

Jimmy Greaves, who missed England's win in the 1966 World Cup final, having been injured during the group stage, had his priorities straight.

★ THE SHELF ★

Liverpool has the Kop, Chelsea has the Shed End, Exeter has the Big Bank – places behind the goal where the most loyal of fans can give their full-throated support for their team. Tottenham have always done things slightly differently, and back in the good old days, the White Hart Lane faithful always wanted to take their place on the Shelf.

Rather than being an area behind the goal, which can sometimes mean that the noise of the fans gets swallowed by the stadium, the Shelf ran the entire length of the White Hart Lane pitch along the East Stand, creating a swell of noise that opposition teams would have been very aware of. In its heyday, 20,000 Spurs fans would be packed on to the two levels of the Shelf.

The Shelf was built during the 1934 refurbishment of White Hart Lane, and the noise that it generated struck fear into opposition fans and players for half a century. It was lost in 1988, when the East Stand was redeveloped to include executive suites, and the noise of the crowd was replaced by the noshing of prawn sandwiches and the sipping of refined Chablis. That, as they say, is progress.

TOTTENHAM WAS THE FIRST BRITISH CLUB TO WIN A MAJOR EUROPEAN COMPETITION, BRINGING HOME THE EUROPEAN CUP WINNERS' CUP IN 1963.

★ PAT JENNINGS ★

Pat Jennings joined Tottenham in 1964 and went on to make 472 league appearances over 13 years. His time guarding the goalmouth saw the team win the FA Cup in 1967, the League Cup in 1971 and 1973, and the UEFA Cup in 1972. He was named the Football Writers' Association's Footballer of the Year in 1973.

By 1977, it was thought that he was nearing the end of his playing career. He left Tottenham and joined Arsenal – where he enjoyed a mere eight more seasons at the top level, taking part in several finals and becoming the first player in English football to make 1,000 senior appearances.

He also turned out for Northern Ireland for 22 years, getting his first cap alongside George Best in 1964 and becoming the oldest player to pull on a national shirt at a World Cup in 1986.

He was welcomed back to Spurs, though, becoming a goalkeeping coach in 1993 and was still a common presence on the training pitches well into his 70s.

With 590 appearances in all competitions, Jennings is the third most-capped Tottenham player after Steve Perryman (854) and Gary Mabbutt (611).

★ SICK AS A PARROT ★

As a society, there are many things that we don't fully understand, but one of the questions that has nagged at academics for over a century is the origin of the phrase 'sick as a parrot'. It's a phrase that has echoed down the generations, uttered by heartbroken managers on football highlights shows since the very day that football highlights shows were first brought into creation.

It's never been proved, but there is a theory that it was on the hallowed turf of White Hart Lane that the phrase 'sick as a parrot' was used in public for the first time.

In 1909, Tottenham Hotspur toured South America. This was a big deal in the days before jumbo jets, and each leg of the journey took three weeks. As a result, strong bonds were formed between the Spurs team (which included an on-trial Walter Tull, see page 16) and the ship's crew. In recognition of these bonds, the captain of the ship gave them the ship's parrot as a gift when they got back to Britain.

The parrot lived happily at White Hart Lane for 11 years, but on the day that the Highbury upstarts took Tottenham's place in the First Division, the parrot is said to have squawked its last and gone off to join the choir invisible, as they say.

Tottenham were as sick as a parrot that day, and the phrase seems to have stuck in footballing circles.

It could be that the introduction of video assistant referees (VAR) will mean that the phrase recedes into the history books because football managers will never again need to complain about a contentious decision made on the football pitch. It's good to live in hope.

CRIMES AGAINST MUSIC:
★ 'DIAMOND LIGHTS' ★

A great song can stand the test of time, becoming something that simultaneously represents a particular place at a particular time and also brings a smile to the faces of people of all ages. Because great music can be eternal.

And then there are other songs: songs that unite people by putting a single-word question into their heads.

And that single-word question is ... 'Why?'

Diamond Lights, a 1987 single by 'Glenn & Chris', sits firmly in the latter category. All but forgotten now, it sits

58

in a dusty corner of the streaming services, unloved and unlistened to. It is a stupendously unimpressive summation of overwrought 1980s synth pop music: plodding, overproduced and inexplicable. Humiliatingly for the people of Great Britain, it reached number 12 in the pop charts, although its follow-up only reached number 92.

But so what? This is a book about the exploits of Tottenham Hotspur, one of the world's most iconic football clubs. Why should anyone care about the forgotten crimes against music committed by Glenn & Chris?

Because Glenn and Chris both had surnames and day jobs. Their surnames were Hoddle and Waddle, and they were two of the most storied players in Spurs' history.

At this point, it is tempting to suggest that you take 30 seconds to listen to the pair's performance on the video-streaming service of your choice ... But know this, curious hunter of the weird and unforgivable, if you search for their content, their numbers will go up and they might reform and do more ...

Darling, I love you, but not that much.

★ MARTIN CHIVERS ★

Martin Chivers, known as Big Chiv, was born in Southampton and joined his local club after writing to them and asking for a trial. It worked, and he made his debut for Southampton at the start of the 1962/63 season at the age of 17. He went on to score 96 goals in 175 appearances.

It is often suggested that players these days don't usually have a say in when they move to a different club – that it's all discussions behind their backs between agents and club scouts. As it turns out, this is not a new phenomenon. Chivers has said that the first he knew of his imminent move from Southampton to Tottenham was when he was walking down the street from the Dell and saw a billboard proclaiming 'Chivers to Spurs'. It's hard to imagine life before mobile phones.

He spent the next eight seasons, from 1968 to 1976, with Spurs, making 278 appearances and scoring 118 times. He spent quite a bit of his first couple of years on the bench, with Jimmy Greaves and Alan Gilzean tending to be favoured, and there were suggestions that he initially had a slightly tense relationship with manager Bill Nicholson. Nevertheless, he stepped up to the plate when Greaves moved on in 1970, scoring 34 times in 58 first team appearances in 1970/71 and then 44 times in 64 appearances the next season.

In total, Chivers delivered 174 goals in 367 appearances for Tottenham, and was Tottenham's leading European goal scorer for nearly 40 years – until Jermain Defoe overtook him in 2013. He also scored 13 goals in 24 appearances for England.

In later years, he was the landlord of a pub in Hatfield, offered his expertise as a radio commentator and regularly returned to White Hart Lane as a match-day host.

★ THE COCKEREL ★

It's easy to imagine that the formation of Tottenham Hotspur and the development of its identity was quick – and that all the elements that we know today were in place within a month. Some of the members of the Tottenham Cricket Club decided that they wanted to form a football team so that they could play sports in the winter, and once they'd made that decision, the name, the kit, the motto and the badge emerged virtually instantaneously.

The reality is more convoluted and quite a lot slower. An example of this is Tottenham's iconic cockerel, which has been central to the club's image seemingly since the dawn of time.

It originally roosted over the West Stand but was moved to the East Stand in the late 1950s to make way for new-fangled floodlights. It's been through a lot has that cockerel, damaged by both the Blitz in World War II and, allegedly, a certain Geordie striker who, in 1988, is said to have decided that it was an excellent target for an air rifle that for some reason he was wandering around with. Probably best not to ask.

It might be a complete coincidence that a year later the original bronze cockerel was given a new home in the Tottenham Hotspur executive offices, with a series of fibreglass replicas put up in its place for the next couple of decades. One assumes they make a less satisfying dink when hit by an air rifle pellet.

The cockerel is so iconic that when Spurs moved into the Tottenham Hotspur Stadium, the original sculpture was scanned using the very latest technology, and an identical replica was cast at nearly twice the size, pellet dents and all. It now perches proudly atop the South Stand.

The thing is, iconic though the cockerel is, the original was not actually created until 1909, Tottenham's inaugural year in the First Division, and did not make it on to Spurs' playing kits for another decade or so. History always has to start somewhere, and that's still more than a century ago now, but there were around 40 years between the club being set up and the cockerel taking pride of place on team shirts.

It's odd to think it, but there's a decent chance that some traditionalist fans were moaning in 1921 about the cockerel being added to the Spurs shirts. Unfortunately, very few online blogs or fan forums from the time survive.

LEAVING THE LANE: ★ FILLING WEMBLEY ★

The decision to leave White Hart Lane was a difficult one, particularly after the 2016/17 season that saw Spurs enjoy second place in the Premier League and go the entire season unbeaten at home for the first time since Jimmy Greaves was wearing the number 10 shirt in 1964/65. The opportunity to build for an even more glorious future awaited though, and with 50,000 people on the waiting list for season tickets, expanding the opportunities for fans to see Tottenham play was imperative.

The only problem was what to do while the new stadium was being built. Rather than go through a season of slightly uncomfortable ground-sharing with one of London's other teams (there are always tensions about who took the last of the milk), the decision was made to decamp to Wembley, England's national stadium.

And so, after 118 years, Tottenham played for the final

time at White Hart Lane on May 14, 2017, brushing aside Manchester United with a 2-1 victory that was never in doubt. There was a certain amount of nervousness on the terraces when Glenn Hoddle and Chris Waddle were announced as part of the half-time entertainment (see page 58). It turned out fine though – they weren't asked to sing – so after one final glorious afternoon, the Tottenham team packed their things and headed 13 miles to the north-west of London.

The original plan was to only play a season at Wembley, but building the Tottenham Hotspur Stadium was a complicated business and, in the end, Spurs were displaced for two seasons. Despite the concern that Wembley might be too big and what can be safely described as a woeful start, the crowds kept coming, breaking attendance records for home matches.

Tottenham found their scoring boots and delivered very respectable third and fourth place finishes in 2017/18 and 2018/19. Attendances remained high, with more than 1.25 million people seeing Spurs during that first season at Wembley – numbers that have broadly held up since the Covid-19 restrictions were lifted. There's an appetite for the Lilywhites.

Player	Club
Michael Owen	Liverpool, Newcastle United, Manchester United, Stoke City
Jermain Defoe	Bournemouth, Sunderland, Tottenham Hotspur, Portsmouth, West Ham, Charlton Athletic
Robbie Fowler	Liverpool, Leeds, Manchester City, Blackburn Rovers
Thierry Henry	Arsenal
Frank Lampard	West Ham, Chelsea, Manchester City
Sergio Agüero	Manchester City
Andrew Cole	Sunderland, Portsmouth, Manchester City, Fulham, Blackburn Rovers, Manchester United, Newcastle United
Wayne Roone	Everton, Manchester United
Harry Kane	Tottenham Hotspur
Alan Shearer	Blackburn Rovers, Newcastle United

Goals

PREMIER LEAGUE'S
★ TOP SCORERS ★

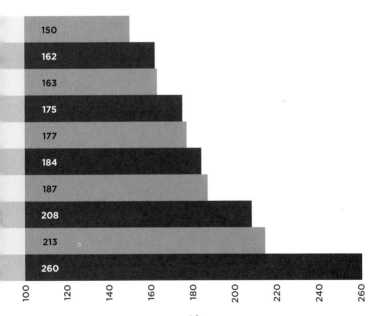

150
162
163
175
177
184
187
208
213
260

100   120   140   160   180   200   220   240   260

THE OPPOSITION: ★ CHELSEA ★

London is full of football teams, and, as one of the most prosperous parts of the United Kingdom, several of those football teams are quite successful.

Chelsea are one of the most successful teams in recent footballing history, and Spurs and Chelsea have been playing each other since 1909. There are rumours that the rivalry between the two teams is based on their proximity, but they can't be that close. According to various online mapping systems and public transport sites, it takes at least an hour to get between the two (although you can get there in 57 minutes by cycling, apparently). No matter what route you take, you won't be going much faster than 10 miles an hour. London's a fast-moving place unless you want to get anywhere.

Anyway, while many rivalries are built up around battles for the top spot, much of the beef between Tottenham and Chelsea is the result of hard-fought battles to avoid relegation from the First to the Second Division in the post-war era (when many of the battles were exceedingly hard fought).

In a lot of ways, though, from Tottenham's point of view, Chelsea is a kind of secondary antagonist. You can't deny that Chelsea often assembles phenomenal teams that are sometimes capable of sublime football, but they are basically there to fill in the time between Arsenal matches. A bit like the Penguin in a Batman film – all good, but most people are waiting for the Joker to show up. Chelsea, bless them, are basically the back-up baddies.

THE BATTLE OF ★ STAMFORD BRIDGE ★

One of the most infamous recent clashes between Tottenham and Chelsea took place in May 2016, where victory would have kept Spurs in contention for the Premier League title. Among the challenges was that Tottenham had not won at Stamford Bridge since 1990.

Despite lifting the trophy the previous year, Chelsea were well out of contention for the title at this point. Like an embittered ex-partner, the west Londoners had made it plain that they would do everything in their power to avoid handing the trophy to the rightful north London heirs at the end of the season.

Tottenham won the first half with goals from Harry Kane and Heung-Min Son. Everything would have been great if the match had stopped there, but unfortunately Chelsea's Gary Cahill and Eden Hazard were having none of it, knocking in two goals during an increasingly bad-tempered second half. The 2–2 draw wasn't enough, and

Spurs were out of the title race.

It became known as the 'Battle of Stamford Bridge' (to the delight of historians everywhere), with 12 yellow cards issued during proceedings, nine of which were brandished at Spurs. The ill discipline also cost Tottenham a considerable sum of money as the Football Association charged them with three counts of failing to control their players and a further sum for receiving more than six yellow cards in a single match. Chelsea were also fined.

While the result was heartbreaking for Tottenham fans around the world, there were several positives to be taken from it.

1. It was Spurs' best Premier League finish at that point.

2. It was nice for Leicester.

3. At least it was Leicester and not anyone else.

4. Yay. Go Leicester!

· TOTTENHAM HOTSPUR ·

★ STEVE PERRYMAN ★

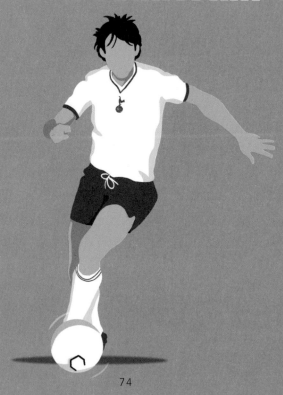

74

· TOTTENHAM HOTSPUR ·

Steve Perryman originally joined Tottenham as a schoolboy in 1967, with legendary manager Bill Nicholson writing him a letter to say that he had never been more pleased to welcome a player to the club. (Perryman still has the letter.)

He made his first team debut two years later, going on to make a record 854 first team appearances for Spurs between 1969 and 1986. He won the League Cup twice, the UEFA Cup twice and captained Tottenham to victory in the FA Cup in 1981 and 1982, when he also received the Football Writers' Association's Footballer of the Year award.

After a successful few years managing Brentford and Watford, Perryman came back to Tottenham as assistant manager when former teammate Ossie Ardiles took on the manager's role, although injuries and internal politics at the club meant that time was never really on their side.

That should not take away from Perryman's central role during a pivotal period for both the club and the game.

TOTTENHAM HOTSPUR ★ STADIUM ★

Tottenham Hotspur opened the doors of its new £1.2 billion stadium to the public in the spring of 2019. The stadium is currently one of the world's most modern footballing venues and boasts the 65-metre Goal Line Bar, the longest bar in Europe that serves what is probably the freshest stadium beer in the world – on account of the oh-so very Shoreditch on-site microbrewery.

The new stadium is state of the art, hosting not only football, but also a range of other entertainment events. This includes American football, with the US National Football League (NFL) agreeing a 10-year deal with Tottenham's owners to hold two games a year at the Tottenham Hotspur Stadium. The stadium's football pitch is retractable, splitting three ways on trays that weigh 3,000 tons and rolling back on 168 wheels powered by 68 motors. It's worth noting that the decision to use 68 motors and 168 wheels was likely to have been a practical engineering decision rather than celebrating a bit of Tottenham magic. Spurs came a modest 7th in the league in 1967/68 and went out in the fifth round of the FA Cup. The shirt number 68 has been used during the Premier League era, not much exciting has ever really happened in it. That said, if you add the numbers six and eight together you end up with 14 (thank us later), which was David Ginola, Gus Poyet and Luka Modrić's shirt number, so it could be related to that ... Practical engineering still seems the most likely reason though. Once the main football pitch is rolled away, the grass is maintained by a complement of robotic lawnmowers and specially developed LED lights that will keep the pitch fit and healthy. It's all very Thunderbirds and means that the Americans can come over to north London, have their fun and not make a mess of the proper football pitch. The process of changing from one pitch to another takes around an hour, so while it all sounds cool and everyone that joins Tottenham is likely to sit and watch it happen once, it's not something that the club has decided to sell tickets for.

Slightly oddly, during Covid-19, when Tottenham was playing behind closed doors, the team decamped from its usual football dressing rooms to the American football dressing rooms because they are larger and, as a result, were easier to use from a social distancing point of view. Presumably, they are larger because they need to accommodate the US players' large shoulder pads and big helmets.

It's not just the NFL that is committed to taking advantage of the Tottenham Hotspur Stadium's phenomenal facilities. Formula 1, the world's pre-eminent motor racing competition, has also recently formed a 15-year strategic partnership with Spurs. The agreement will see go-karting tracks added to the stadium's facilities that will help bring jobs to the local community, unearth drivers of the future, and potentially bring national karting races to the stadium.

It's worth pointing out that back in the early to mid-twentieth century, Chelsea's Stamford Bridge used to host speedway racing, greyhound racing and a host of other activities. Some suggested at the time that Chelsea's leadership was putting revenue generation before football. These are of course different times and this is of course a different club …

The stadium is designed to offer what is called 'quick and clean reverberation times', which basically translates to fans in the stands being more likely to be able to sing in unison because the acoustics are set up in such a way that they can hear people in the neighbouring stands, rather than their echoes. It's certainly come a long way from simply carrying the stands down from Northumberland Park to White Hart Lane.

The heritage of the Lane has not been forgotten, though, with the crushed remains of the old stadium incorporated into both the foundations and the concourses of the new. The jury's out about whether this was sentimentality, environmental consciousness or simply cheaper than getting the old stadium carted away.

All of this has been expensive to deliver, but ticket revenues from the new stadium are expected to be around double what could previously be attracted at White Hart Lane, and returns from other activities are likely to be similarly elevated.

The focus in the development of the Tottenham Hotspur Stadium has been in delivering a phenomenal match-day experience. And it's bigger than either Arsenal or West Ham's new stadiums. Not that that's important.

★ THE SOUTH STAND ★

To be fair to those who still think that White Hart Lane lost its heart when the Shelf was transmogrified into executive boxes in 1988 (see page 53), the designers of the Tottenham Hotspur Stadium have put a lot of thought into the sound design of the new stadium.

The South Stand, the home end reserved for 17,500 of the faithful, is the largest single-tier stand in the country; it is designed to give fans a focal point and create an intimidating wall of sound when Spurs are playing at home.

The entire stadium is designed to funnel sound back on to the pitch, encouraging Tottenham's players to perform to the very best of their abilities.

Rumours that the South Stand has been earmarked for redevelopment into executive boxes by 2035 are probably completely untrue.

TECHNOLOGY THAT MAKES GRASS ⋆ GROWING EXCITING ⋆

People like to talk about the hallowed turf of a stadium, but these days there's a lot of science that goes with the magic, particularly where the Tottenham Hotspur Stadium is concerned.

Once the match is over and the fans have gone home, the silence of the stadium is broken by the wheeling out of a 120-tonne lighting system with 863 LED lights that ensures each blade of grass grows just so. This being the Tottenham Hotspur Stadium, it's safe to assume that the silence is only slightly broken because the whole lighting system moves with barely a whisper.

Apparently, there's one part of the mechanism that squeaks ever so slightly but no one has yet been able to track it down and get some 3-in-1 oil on it.

★ THE GAP ★

Football is built around a simple concept: whoever gets the most points wins the season. There are thousands of little battles, but when you look back at the whole thing, the primary question is: Who got the most points?

After that, if you are not the team that gets the most points, the questions become a little wider: How many points did the winner take, and how many points did my team take? The gap between the two tells you whether a team was in the running or simply taking up space in the League.

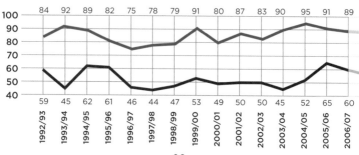

82

In the case of Tottenham, on average, they have been 28 points off the pace during the Premier League years. Given the significant improvement there has been in the Tottenham league positions over the last decade or so (see page 14), over the last 10 years they have only been 22 points off the pace. However, if you look at the last five years, Spurs have been around 27 points off the pace. To be fair, though, the number of points required to win the Premier League has also risen – from 88 points since 1992/93 to 95 points on average over the last five years, which pretty much correlates.

Ultimately, the trend with Tottenham has been heading in the right direction, but winning a top-flight title is never going to be anything other than incredibly difficult.

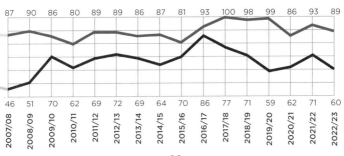

87	90	86	80	89	89	86	87	81	93	100	98	99	86	93	89
46	51	70	62	69	72	69	64	70	86	77	71	59	62	71	60

2007/08 · 2008/09 · 2009/10 · 2010/11 · 2011/12 · 2012/13 · 2013/14 · 2014/15 · 2015/16 · 2016/17 · 2017/18 · 2018/19 · 2019/20 · 2020/21 · 2021/22 · 2022/23

★ OSSIE ARDILES ★

84

Where to start with Osvaldo César Ardiles? The fact that he was widely known as 'Ossie' is a good place to start, but that doesn't really need much in the way of explanation. He was Argentinian, which was a politically challenging thing to be in Britain in the early to mid-1980s when we briefly went to war with the South American dictatorship for reasons that are entirely too convoluted to go into here.

He joined Tottenham just after the 1978 World Cup, and stayed at White Hart Lane for 10 seasons, although he went out on loan for the majority of the 1982/83 season as a result of the Falklands War. During his time as a Spurs player, he won the FA Cup twice and the UEFA Cup as well as sharing the honours for the Charity Shield.

In all, he played for Tottenham 238 times and went on to manage the team in 1993; however, despite some big signings, he failed to make much of an impression and was moved on relatively quickly.

CRIMES AGAINST MUSIC: 'OSSIE'S DREAM (SPURS ARE ON THEIR ★ WAY TO WEMBLEY)' ★

Ossie Ardiles' greatest contribution to British society is the role he played in *Ossie's Dream (Spurs are on Their Way to Wembley)* by the Tottenham Hotspur FA Cup Final Squad and Chas & Dave. Released to celebrate Tottenham reaching the FA Cup final in 1981, it reached number 5 in the UK singles chart.

By all accounts, Ardiles does not have a particular problem with pronouncing the word 'Tottenham', but was willing to step up to the mike and utter the immortal line, 'In de cup for Totting-ham' for no apparent reason other than it seemed like a good idea when someone suggested it in the recording studio because, 'Cor blimey, strike a light, don't them foreigners talk funny.' In fact, he spent many years trying to disassociate himself from the song, although he appears to have mellowed towards it as the years have gone by (and, presumably, people have stopped asking about it).

The other notable thing about the song is that the single was available in record shops around north London within 48 hours of being recorded. This may not sound massively impressive in these days of streamed downloads, but, at the time, physical vinyl had to be pressed and the resulting records put in a van and provided to actual record shops. So, producing and distributing it in two days was, in many ways, a more impressive feat than the actual record itself.

It's fair to say that the song is quite annoying and liable to get lodged in your head once you've heard it – although it's not actually excruciating … it's just a completely forgettable piece of music that's impossible to forget. This may or may not be a compliment.

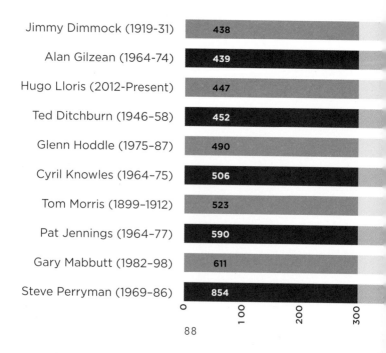

Jimmy Dimmock (1919-31) — 438

Alan Gilzean (1964-74) — 439

Hugo Lloris (2012-Present) — 447

Ted Ditchburn (1946-58) — 452

Glenn Hoddle (1975-87) — 490

Cyril Knowles (1964-75) — 506

Tom Morris (1899-1912) — 523

Pat Jennings (1964-77) — 590

Gary Mabbutt (1982-98) — 611

Steve Perryman (1969-86) — 854

TOTTENHAM'S TOP TEN FIRST TEAM ★ APPEARANCES ★

(ALL COMPETITIONS)

300 400 500 600 700 800 900

★ PAUL GASCOIGNE ★

Paul Gascoigne was a joy to watch on the football pitch, bossing the midfield and making runs that struck fear into the opposition. His deftness of touch meant you never knew where he was going next.

He was also famous for his antics off the pitch (see page 64), which started out as endearing but slowly started to make headlines for the wrong reasons. In the 1990s, the British media used every possible means to build people up so that they could knock them down – and in Gascoigne's case, they succeeded spectacularly.

He played 92 times for Spurs between 1988 and 1992, although he spent the entire 1991/92 season out with a knee injury (with his recovery allegedly slowed down after a non-football-related incident at a night club). He left White Hart Lane for Lazio, where he stayed for three seasons.

He played 57 times for England, scoring 10 goals, one of which led to possibly the most unlikely/cheeky/notorious/tabloid-baiting (delete as appropriate) goal celebration in English football history. It involved a dentist's chair.

CRIMES AGAINST MUSIC: ★ 'FOG ON THE TYNE' ★

It's possible that he was inspired by Glenn & Chris; it's possible that he did it as a dare; it's possible that he thought he could bring even more joy to the world through his music than he did as a superlative talent on the football field. Whatever the reason (or whatever the excuse), in 1990, Paul Gascoigne, Tottenham's mercurial attacking midfielder, decided that it would be a good idea to unleash his rendition of *Fog on the Tyne* on an unsuspecting, and perhaps undeserving, world.

Fog on the Tyne was originally released in the early 1970s by Lindisfarne, a Newcastle-based folk-rock band. It's a pleasant folk ditty, steeped in the unique perspective of the north-east of England. It really didn't deserve the addition of a 1980s drum machine, a synth solo and one of the greatest midfield talents that this country has ever produced inexplicably saying, "Come on" repeatedly.

It also has a 12" remix, apparently, but nobody has the courage to listen to it. The best thing you can say about it is that at least they all appear to be having a jolly nice time.

SPURS WERE THE FIRST CLUB TO WIN THE LEAGUE CUP AT THE NEW WEMBLEY (2007/08).

CELEBS ON THE
★ TERRACE ★

As is natural for a north London club that is exceptionally well connected, Spurs have several famous fans.

Four stars of the Marvel firmament have publicly expressed their devotion to Tottenham: Dave Bautista (Drax in *Guardians of the Galaxy*), Tom Holland (Spider-Man himself), Kenneth Branagh (director, *Thor*) and Jude Law (Yon-Rogg in *Captain Marvel*). Tom Hardy (who stars as Eddie Brock in the *Venom* films, which are associated with, but not really part of, the Marvel Cinematic Universe, because, sweet Lord, if you thought that the early years of football were complicated, you should try tracking the film rights to Marvel comic characters from the 1990s onwards) has never publicly proclaimed his allegiance, despite narrating a recent documentary about Spurs. Chris Evans is also said to be a fan, although that's British Chris Evans the radio presenter and television personality, rather than American Chris Evans who played both Captain America and the *Fantastic Four*'s Johnny Storm (because, sweet

Lord, if you thought that the early years of football were complicated, you should try to keep track of the actors that have played roles in Marvel films down the years).

In the world of music, Adele is the big draw and Mark Wahlberg has been known to pull on a Lilywhite shirt. Chas & Dave obviously deserve a mention, but various members of rock band Def Leppard, even rockier band UFO, and grebo band the incredible Pop Will Eat Itself are known to be supporters of the club. There's a hierarchy of obscurity in there somewhere.

Ron Weasley actor Rupert Grint has also been sorted into Spurs and stated that his great-grandfather had a box at White Hart Lane. Could it be that a forebear of a member of the Gryffindor Three was responsible for the mysterious disappearance of the Shelf at White Hart Lane (see page 53)? Somewhere, tucked away in a dusty tome in a corner of the Hogwarts library, there might be an answer ... (although it's more likely that the answer can be found tucked away on a dusty spreadsheet in a cheap plastic folder on a shelf in an accountant's office somewhere on an industrial estate in the suburbs of north London. Sorry to ruin the magic.)

★ GARY LINEKER ★

Gary Lineker joined Tottenham Hotspur after stints at
Leicester City, Everton and Barcelona, bringing with him a
reputation as a prolific striker. Lineker did the right thing,
signed for Spurs and lived up to his reputation, finding
the back of the net 80 times in 138 appearances over
three seasons across all competitions. He was the First
Division's highest scorer in 1989/90 and second highest
scorer in 1991/92.

He'd worked with Terry Venables at Barcelona, helping
them win the Spanish Cup (The Copa del Rey) and the
European Cup Winners' Cup, and rejoined Venables at
Tottenham, allegedly rebuffing the advances of the then-
emerging Manchester United manager Alex Ferguson.

Lineker helped Tottenham win the FA Cup in 1991, the
eighth time the team had lifted the trophy – which at that
point was an English record. The team had beaten Arsenal
in the semi-final, with Lineker scoring twice (see page
29) to put an end to the Gunners' dreams of a domestic
double.

Lineker had a reputation as a nice guy, and did not receive
a red card at any point in his 16-year career. To be fair,
though, Chelsea hard man Ron 'Chopper' Harris also made

it through his career without being sent off, so perhaps it's not such a great gauge.

After leaving Spurs, Lineker joined Nagoya Grampus Eight, although his two seasons in Japan were blighted by injury and he ended his playing career there.

He has gone on to become *Match of the Day*'s longest-serving anchor, as well as heading up the BBC's coverage of international football tournaments. He also led a campaign to save Leicester City from bankruptcy, helped flog a few bags of crisps and has become increasingly vocal on social media. These are good things if you come from Leicester, enjoy potato snacks or agree with his opinions.

WHEN ALAN SUGAR GAVE 114% TO ENGLISH FOOTBALL

Before Sir Alan Sugar became the face of the annual business pantomime and cliché-spouting pillock parade *The Apprentice*, he was a well-connected, vaguely credible 1980s man of business who saved Tottenham Hotspur Football Club and changed the very face of English football as we know it.

By the end of the 1980s, a lot of football clubs were in trouble. Hooliganism on the terraces was keeping a lot of people away from matches and had seen all English clubs banned from European competitions – both of which had a chilling effect on revenues. Stamford Bridge was under threat of being improved by being turned into a supermarket and housing estate, and Spurs were in debt to the tune of more than £10 million, which was a considerable sum at the time.

Step forward Sir Alan, who teamed up with Terry Venables to sort things out. Between them, they added some cash to the business to keep the creditors from the door, bought players – including Lineker and Gascoigne – and brought some tactical nous on to the pitch. Victory in the FA Cup followed and the future looked bright.

Meanwhile, the TV contracts were up for review, with ITV looking like they were going to secure broadcasting rights. There was a decent deal on the table, with the era's big five teams – Arsenal, Everton, Liverpool, Manchester United and Spurs – taking the lion's share of the spoils and the rest being shared between the other teams.

At the last minute in the negotiations, Sir Alan, who's company supplied Sky with the satellite dishes that customers needed to receive satellite broadcasts at the time, is said to have stepped out of the room to make a quick personal phone call. Shortly afterwards, and possibly by complete coincidence, Sky representatives came back into the negotiations with an offer that was said to have blown ITV's offer out of the water.

The two deals are said to have been put to a vote, and while Sir Alan offered to abstain due to his relationship with Sky, he was allowed to cast a vote and the Sky bid won the day (there is slightly more information about the whole thing available than there was about the incident in 1919).

It was a multimillion-pound deal that led indirectly to the formation of the Premier League.

The relationship between Venables and Sugar soured and ultimately ended up in court, but, for a brief moment in time, they had combined to save Spurs and change the face of English football. It's almost enough to forgive another series of *The Apprentice*.

THE
★ TOTTENHAM CAKE ★

Available at reputable bakers up and down the country and served at special events at Tottenham Hotspur Football Club, the Tottenham cake originally had religious, rather than footballing, associations. It was created by the Quakers, a protestant group that moved to the Tottenham area in search of a rural way of life away from the distractions of the city. To be fair to them, this was in the 17th century.

The cake itself is a simple traybake, topped by distinctive pink icing, which was achieved by crushing mulberries that grew in the grounds of the local Quaker Meeting House. By the end of the 19th century, Tottenham cake could be bought for a penny a square (or ha'penny for a half square), offering an affordable treat for people around the borough.

The association between club and cake was baked in 1901, when Tottenham beat Sheffield United 3–1 to win the FA Cup and local bakers handed out squares of the cake free to local children in celebration.

TOTTENHAM HOTSPUR WERE ORIGINALLY CALLED HOTSPUR FC, BUT CHANGED THEIR NAME TO TOTTENHAM HOTSPUR IN 1884 TO AVOID CONFUSION WITH ANOTHER LOCAL CLUB LONDON HOTSPUR.

★ SOL CAMPBELL ★

'Time heals wounds,' they say, and now, two decades on, it's probably time to accept Sol Campbell's decision to leave Spurs and go somewhere three miles away while he was at the top of his game.

A robust defender, Campbell joined Tottenham's youth set-up after a brief spell at West Ham. He was ambitious and driven, and even turned down the England Youth team's captain's armband because he wanted to focus on his own game.

He quite illustriously marked his first team debut in 1992 with Tottenham by scoring against Chelsea and was instrumental in the team reaching the semi-finals of the 1994/95 FA Cup. He rose to the position of club captain shortly afterwards.

Despite his contributions, it appears that Campbell did not have a great relationship with many of the carousel of managers that Tottenham endured during the latter half of the 1990s, and it could be argued that he received a lack of support from the club with issues off the pitch. Either way, when his contract expired in the summer of 2001, despite there being an extension on the table, he made the decision to move on from White Hart Lane.

It's a real shame that Campbell is remembered for moving across north London rather than his contributions to Tottenham while he was at White Hart Lane. The Spurs community has been subject to some extremely unpleasant racial abuse down the years, and it feels like sometimes, when the subject of Campbell comes up, some fans have been quick to sink to that level.

In the end, he was a stalwart of the Tottenham defence for over 10 years, was captain for the club and the country and he should be remembered with respect.

SPURS WERE FIRST TEAM TO TIE THEIR COLOURS TO THE FA CUP TROPHY IN CELEBRATION, A TRADITION WHICH HAS REMAINED EVER SINCE.

TOTTENHAM HOTSPUR ★ FC WOMEN ★

It's wrong to talk about Tottenham without recognising the existence of the women's team. Formed in 1985 as Broxbourne Ladies, the team received permission to become Tottenham Hotspur Ladies FC for the 1991/92 season.

The team is a relative newcomer to the top flight of women's football, taking on professional status in the 2017/18 season, but with a growing fan base and a clearly defined development pathway, the club has a strong future.

It's a funny old thing, but there's probably more information around about the formation of Tottenham's men's team 130 years ago than there is about the women's team 30 years ago. Now, though, with the England team lifting the Women's European Cup in 2022, and the Tottenham team building a solid and consistent presence in the top flight of women's football in England, it seems likely that the focus on the team will increase.

For those who are sniffy about the women's game, it is worth pointing out that it has been played for around as long as the men's game. The first men's international game was played in 1872 and watched by an estimated 4,000 people, while a series of women's internationals between England and Scotland nine years later are said to have attracted crowds of up to 5,000 people. There's a certain amount of comparing apples and pears in this, and the historical information is sketchy to say the least, but these women's matches were set up by private companies and were intended to generate revenue, so they probably wouldn't have happened if they didn't make money.

Away from the glamorous trendsetting of the 19th century international footballer, some clubs in England started letting women in to matches for free as a way of reducing crowd trouble. The move briefly caught on until someone worked out that watching football was a popular pastime for both sexes – and the clubs were losing out on quite a bit of gate money by letting women in gratis.

While men's football was curtailed during World War I, the women's game continued and is said to have made considerable charitable contributions throughout the post-war period. Unfortunately, this popularity meant that the gentlemen of the Football Association started to feel threatened by female success and made moves to stub the game out – on the grounds that it wasn't good for women's physical or moral health.

There's no suggestion that Spurs or anyone associated with the team had anything particular to do with this specific decision, or with women's football generally prior to the 1990s, but it seems like the club is making up for it now.

Player	Club
Bryan Robson	West Bromwich Albion, Manchester United, Middlesborough
Billy Wright	Wolverhampton Wanderers
Frank Lampard	West Ham, Chelsea, Manchester City
Bobby Charlton	Manchester United
Ashley Cole	Arsenal, Chelsea, Derby County
Bobby Moore	West Ham, Fulham
Steven Gerrard	Liverpool
David Beckham	Manchester United
Wayne Rooney	Everton, Manchester United, Derby County
Peter Shilton	Leicester City, Stoke City, Nottingham Forest, Southampton, Derby County, Plymouth Argyle, Wimbledon, Bolton Wanderers, Coventry City, West Ham United, Leyton Orient

Caps

ENGLAND CAPS
CAPS
★ **CHART** ★

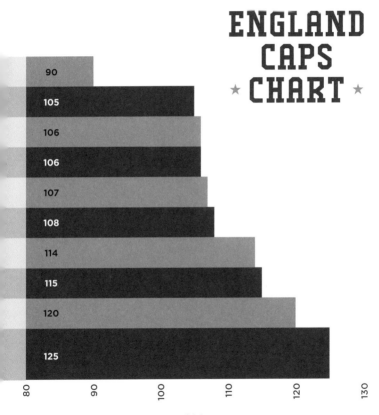

90	
105	
106	
106	
107	
108	
114	
115	
120	
125	

80 90 100 110 120 130

★ TEDDY SHERINGHAM ★

When you look at the list of Tottenham goal scorers in the Premier League era, Teddy Sheringham's name stands out. Gracing the Tottenham team with two spells during his career, Walthamstow-born Sheringham is third only to Harry Kane and Heung-Min Son in front of goal for Spurs in the Premier League.

He was the top scorer in the Premier League's inaugural season, scoring one goal with Nottingham Forest (which was, incidentally, the first live goal shown on the fledgeling Sky Sports) before doing the sensible thing and joining Spurs, where he proceeded to knock in 21 goals that season. He left Spurs in 1997 to go and get rained on for four years, before seeing sense and returning to White Hart Lane for a couple more seasons, making 70 more Premier League appearances and delivering 22 more goals.

He was also a mainstay of the England team, scoring 11 times for his 51 appearances for the Three Lions and providing a vital qualifying goal within 15 seconds of being on the pitch against Greece in 2001.

He's kept himself busy closing the book on his playing days, playing poker to a high level, doing a bit of football management and warbling for public approval as the performing tree on *The Masked Singer*.

THE OPPOSITION:
★ LIVERPOOL ★

Tottenham's rivalry with Liverpool does not really extend beyond a strictly professional distaste for one another. There have been some tasty clashes between the two down the years, but never anything that translated into long-term tension.

There have been players that have played for both teams, but, in the main, they make their way up or down the M1 with little animosity. In the case of Robbie Keane, his time on Merseyside was limited, with Tottenham welcoming him back in the January transfer window for around £7 million less than Liverpool had purchased him for in the previous September. A nice bit of business, no hard feelings.

Football is full of legendary rivalries that echo down the generations. Family tales of grandparents that won't sit together for a Sunday roast because one wears blue and the other proudly bares the black and white stripes. Fables of two households, both alike in dignity, who are always quick to break ancient grudge into new mutiny ... Liverpool and Tottenham are not really like that.

Although obviously, "O Crouchio, Crouchio, wherefore art thou Crouchio?"

★ MANAGERS' TIMELINE ★

Tottenham have enjoyed the services of around 20 managers since the Premier League was formed three decades ago, each of them bringing their unique skills and experiences to the team. On average, they last around 20 months, a little over a season and a half, although caretaker managers who pitch in for a handful of games bring this average down.

Basically, they tend to have around two seasons before the chairman wields the axe by mutual consent.

Season	Month hired	Manager
1992/93	Aug-92	Doug Livermore Ray Clemence
1993/94	Aug-93	Osvaldo Ardiles
1994/95	Oct-94	Steve Perryman
1994/95	Nov-94	Gerry Francis
1996/97	Dec-96	Christian Gross
1998/99	Sep-98	David Pleat
1998/99	Nov-98	George Graham
2000/01	Mar-01	Glenn Hoddle
2003/04	Oct-03	David Pleat
2003/04	Jun-04	Jacques Santini
2004/05	Dec-04	Martin Jol
2007/08	Nov-07	Juande Ramos
2008/09	Nov-08	Harry Redknapp
2011/12	Jul-12	André Villas-Boas
2013/14	Jan-14	Tim Sherwood
2013/14	Jun-14	Mauricio Pochettino
2019/20	Dec-19	José Mourinho
2020/21	May-21	Ryan Mason
2020/21	Jun-21	Nuno Espírito Santo
2021/22	Nov-21	Antonio Conte

"TOTTENHAM ARE TRYING TONIGHT TO BECOME THE FIRST LONDON TEAM TO WIN THIS CUP. THE LAST TEAM TO DO SO WAS THE 1973 SPURS TEAM."

Mike Ingham, British football commentator, forgets that Spurs have historically always played at the same stadium as Tottenham, and that stadium has always been in north London.

"I'M NOT GOING TO MAKE THE SAME MISTAKES. I'LL MAKE NEW MISTAKES."

So said José Mourinho at his first press conference as Tottenham head coach. He was half right; he went on to make several new mistakes alongside a slew of the same mistakes.

THE OPPOSITION:
★ MANCHESTER UNITED ★

Manchester United has been on a pedestal for 25 of the last 30 years, dominating football both domestically and internationally, and having a decent shout at claiming to be one of the world's three biggest clubs.

Their return to mortality has been gratifying for every other team in the world. It proves that there is not something in the water at Trafford Park; they have simply created a string of superlative teams through exceptional strategies and hard work. Which means that their success can be emulated.

There is no particular tension between Manchester United and Spurs, but given United's dominance in the majority of the Premier League seasons between 1992/93 and 2012/13, it's probably best to draw a veil over the stats and simply doff a cap in the direction of the red part of Manchester. Perhaps we can go back to the spreadsheets once the 2032/33 season is completed – when, hopefully, the statistics will be a little more even.

FORMER CAPTAIN AND DEFENDER LEDLEY KING SCORED IN 9.9 SECONDS AGAINST BRADFORD CITY, WHICH AT THE TIME WAS THE FASTEST GOAL EVER SCORED IN THE PREMIER LEAGUE.

JÜRGEN
★ KLINSMANN ★

World Cup winner Jürgen Klinsmann's stay at White Hart Lane was relatively brief, but the fans were quick to take to the self-deprecating German. Arriving from Monaco with a reputation as someone who, perhaps, suffered from gravity a little more than most other people on the planet, he scored with his head on his debut – and then celebrated by taking a theatrical dive with a broad grin all over his face.

He went on to score 21 goals for Tottenham in the 1994/95 season and 30 goals in all competitions. He also received the 1995 Football Writers' Association's Footballer of the Year award.

It was, as they say, a brief affair, though, and by the next season he had moved on to Germany and then Italy. He returned briefly to the Lane in 1997, where he contributed nine goals in 15 games to help save the club from relegation.

There were those at the time who questioned why the great German wanted to come to north London, but the word on the street is that he didn't like the approach that his manager at Monaco was taking. That manager was Arsène Wenger.

★ ST HOTSPUR DAY ★
II

Statistically, it would take quite a large piece of paper, a decent chunk of time and an impressive understanding of maths to work out the odds of Spurs facing Arsenal on a specific day in any given football season. Even without the precise odds (which can potentially be estimated to be somewhere in the region between 50,710,635 to one and 43 to one, probably no more or less), it is perhaps surprising that Tottenham faced Arsenal once again (see page 29) on St Hotspur Day, 14th April, in 2010.

Arsenal needed to beat Spurs to keep their title hopes alive, so the result was never really in doubt. The match saw Danny Rose score his debut goal, a volley from outside the box that looped over the Arsenal defence and buried itself in the back of the net. A pre-ponytailed Gareth Bale doubled the lead, scoring his first goal of the season and bringing delight to the terraces of White Hart Lane.

Someone or other pulled one back for Arsenal, but it wasn't enough, and Spurs fans were forced to endure the sad, sad sight of a demoralised Arsène Wenger and his team trudging dejectedly back to the away dressing rooms at the end of the match. Some of the more thoughtful Spurs fans may have sung some songs to cheer up the south London team and its fans as they made their way out into the crisp spring night, but it was probably in vain.

Still, it was nice of them to try.

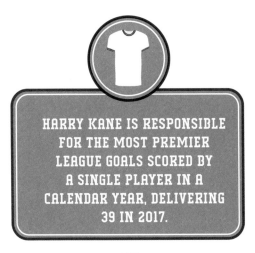

HARRY KANE IS RESPONSIBLE FOR THE MOST PREMIER LEAGUE GOALS SCORED BY A SINGLE PLAYER IN A CALENDAR YEAR, DELIVERING 39 IN 2017.

THE OPPOSITION:
★ MANCHESTER CITY ★

Manchester City's rise has regularly been described as meteoric. Before 2009/10, the blue side of Manchester were used to doing the yo-yo alongside Norwich, Huddersfield, Burnley and the like. Sometimes they were in the Premier League, sometimes they were elsewhere. One quick takeover and a heathy injection of cash later, and Manchester City have been transformed into one of the biggest teams in the world.

Spurs, of course, have been on their own journey in that time, but the two teams seem, in the main, to have rubbed along quite nicely together. Tottenham versus Manchester City is always a hard-fought match, but it's rarely particularly salty.

Their history stretches right the way back to their first official meeting in 1909, when Spurs put City out of the FA Cup, but honours have been pretty even in the century since. They've both won 66 of the 168 matches they've played in all competitions, and shared the points in the remaining 36. The dial has shifted slightly since 2009, with Manchester City winning 53% of the encounters, but they've only won four of the last 10 up to the end of the 2022/23 season.

The nice thing about statistics is that they can be made to tell you anything you like.

"I OFTEN THINK THAT INSTEAD OF SPENDING 10 YEARS WORRYING ABOUT CARLOS KICKABALL ON THE PITCH AND GETTING CRITICISED BY THE FANS, I COULD HAVE DONE SOMETHING MORE LUCRATIVE. I WAS STILL A YOUNG MAN THEN."

Sir Alan Sugar reflects on his time as Spurs chairman, while the rest of us breathe a sigh of relief that it meant he didn't have time to unleash another Amstrad product on the world.

"THERE'S ALWAYS BEEN
A FIERCE RIVALRY
BETWEEN SPURS AND
TOTTENHAM."

David Pleat, English footballer
and manager, proves that in
football, sometimes the toughest
battle is against yourself.

★ GARETH BALE ★

Gareth Bale is widely regarded as one of the greatest players of his generation and one of the greatest Welsh players of all time. There's not really much more to say, really, but we'll carry on anyway ...

Bale's ability was apparent from a young age, with his school PE teacher allowing him to play football only if he committed to taking one touch and not using his left foot.

Like Martin Chivers, Bale started his career at Southampton, where he made 40 appearances in the 2006/07 season, scoring five goals, before attracting the attention of Tottenham, where he transformed himself from a left back and free-kick specialist into a winger with an absolutely devastating free-kick ability.

On his third appearance for Tottenham, a home match at White Hart Lane at the start of the 2007/08 season, he stepped up and stroked a beautiful, low, curling free kick into the bottom left of the Arsenal goal; a phenomenal piece of skill that brings a smile to the face every time.

While he suffered several injuries and spent time on the sidelines through surgery, his talent shone when he was on the field. In the 2012/13 season, he won the Professional Footballers' Association Players' Player of the Year, the

Young Player of the Year award, and the Football Writers' Association's Footballer of the Year Award, becoming one of only two players to have won all three awards in the same season (the other being Cristiano Ronaldo in 2007).

At that point, a major talent had officially arrived and it became a question of when, rather than if, he was going to leave; sure enough, in September 2013, Bale moved to Spain to join Real Madrid.

It's fair to say that his time with the Spanish giants wasn't without controversy, but he continued to be a major presence on the pitch whenever he played, winning La Liga three times and the UEFA Champions' League five times. He returned to Spurs briefly on loan for the 2020/21 season, adding 11 goals in 20 appearances to his goal tally from his first Spurs stint of 42 in 146 appearances, before having a final year in Spain and then finishing his professional career with a year playing for Los Angeles FC.

Bale was the youngest player to play for Wales on his debut in 2006 (although his record was beaten by Harry Wilson in 2013). He played more than 100 times for his country and played a leading role in helping Wales qualify for the 2022 World Cup – the first time they had achieved this since 1958 – as well as the Euros in 2016 and 2020.

"GARETH BALE LITERALLY HAS THREE LUNGS."

Jamie Redknapp proves that we really need to talk more openly about the definition of the word literally. Unless Bale is from considerably further away than Wales, Literally.

CRIMES AGAINST MUSIC: ★ 'NICE ONE CYRIL' ★

Tottenham's dalliance with musical notoriety existed long before anyone inexplicably suggested that Gascoigne, Hoddle or Waddle should be allowed anywhere within 100 metres of a recording studio.

In the early 1970s, there was a group called the Cockerel Chorus that delivered two kinds of songs: cheeky, cheery folk classics and cheeky, cheery songs sung in homage to Tottenham Hotspur. One of their albums was called *Party Sing-A-Long*, which boasted a cover of quite hairy people in flared jeans and nylon shirts looking like they were having a super fun time.

One of the songs that the Cockerel Chorus produced was called *Nice One Cyril*, sung in honour of the era's tenacious left back, Cyril Knowles. The song evolved from an advert for Wonderloaf Bread, which congratulated a baker called Cyril for his superlative bread. Wonderloaf had a bakery within sniffing distance of White Hart Lane, and Tottenham had a defender called Cyril, so *Nice one Cyril* was quickly adopted on the terraces.

The song was given an ambitious operatic opening that was, presumably, very rarely imitated on the terraces on a Saturday afternoon, but which romps along in a perfectly pleasant early 1970s fashion (cheerily and cheekily). It reached number 14 in the hit parade at around the same time as Tottenham lifted the League Cup in 1973. Pub quiz trivia fans might also wish to note that the single also includes the unlikely professional debut of one Nicko McBrain, who went on to become Iron Maiden's drummer.

Over recent years, *Nice One Cyril* has once again echoed around the Tottenham terraces, adapted to honour forward Heung-Min Son: 'Nice one Sonny, Nice one Son, Nice one Sonny, Let's have another one.'

And he usually obliges.

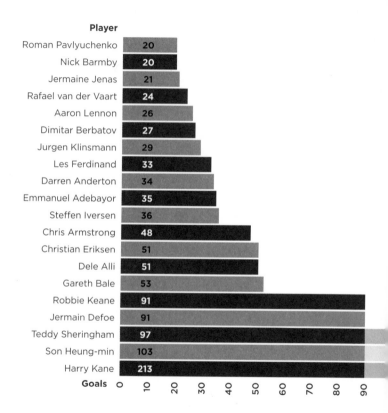

Player

Player	Goals
Roman Pavlyuchenko	20
Nick Barmby	20
Jermaine Jenas	21
Rafael van der Vaart	24
Aaron Lennon	26
Dimitar Berbatov	27
Jurgen Klinsmann	29
Les Ferdinand	33
Darren Anderton	34
Emmanuel Adebayor	35
Steffen Iversen	36
Chris Armstrong	48
Christian Eriksen	51
Dele Alli	51
Gareth Bale	53
Robbie Keane	91
Jermain Defoe	91
Teddy Sheringham	97
Son Heung-min	103
Harry Kane	213

Goals 0 10 20 30 40 50 60 70 80 90

TOTTENHAM'S LEADING PREMIER LEAGUE ★ GOAL SCORERS ★

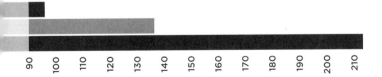

90 100 110 120 130 140 150 160 170 180 190 200 210

★ LUKA MODRIĆ ★

Luka Modrić joined Tottenham in 2008 as the first of Juande Ramos' many summer signings. The Dinamo Zagreb midfielder was also attracting attention from Newcastle and Manchester City, so there were high hopes that attracting his signature would help Spurs enjoy a good year in the Premier League.

He struggled initially, though, with an early injury leading to questions about whether he could take the robust pace of the Premier League. He was also regularly played out of position before the arrival of Harry Redknapp saw him put into his preferred central or left midfield positions.

He became a central part of the Spurs set-up during the next three years, attracting admiring comments and the occasional offer from some of the other big clubs in the Premier League. Chelsea were unsubtle in their pursuit, although Modrić's suggestion that he had a gentleman's agreement with the Tottenham chairman that he could leave if a 'big club' came knocking might not have been the most subtle way of giving the Blues the brush-off. Or he might have been flirting.

In the end, he moved to Real Madrid for the 2012/13 season after seeming to become increasingly unsettled in the Premier League. He has thrived in Spain and become one of the most admired and respected players of his generation. He has also taken part in nine international tournaments with the Croatian national team.

He scored 13 goals in 127 appearances for Tottenham's first team, and has gone on to win some of the highest honours in football with Real Madrid, including La Liga three times and the UEFA Champions League no less than five times. Looking at his subsequent career, it's difficult not to think about Modrić's four years with Spurs, excellent though they were, and wonder what might have been ...

MODRIĆ WAS NAMED IN THE EURO 2016 AND WORLD CUP 2018 REFUGEE XIS, AS A RESULT OF BEING FORCED TO FLEE HIS CHILDHOOD HOME IN THE CROATIAN WAR OF INDEPENDENCE.

"SOCCER IS A GAME FOR 22 PEOPLE THAT RUN AROUND, PLAY THE BALL, AND ONE REFEREE WHO MAKES A SLEW OF MISTAKES, AND IN THE END GERMANY ALWAYS WINS,"

proclaimed Gary Lineker once upon a time. Gloriously he had to update it after Germany crashed out of the 2022 World Cup. Didn't really help England though.

THE OPPOSITION:
★ WEST HAM ★

There are crunch matches with Liverpool, the Manchesters or some brief meteor like Leicester or Newcastle that light up the Premier League for a season or so, there are long-term grudge matches with our good friends in west London and neighbours in north London ... and then there are the matches with West Ham.

Let's be clear here: in the same way that Tottenham have Arsenal, West Ham save their real passion for matches against their neighbours Millwall, but with the assertive south Londoners tending to lurk in the lower leagues in recent years, West Ham are inclined to see playing Tottenham as a derby day.

Tottenham, in turn, have tended to see West Ham as a feisty little brother – in some ways, not unlike Scrappy Doo. The east London team can be noisy and are perfectly capable of causing an upset, but when it happens it is an upset rather than an even clash of two mighty titans of football. For this reason, Spurs fans are likely to refer to games with the Hammers as 'West Ham's Cup Final'.

West Ham have not finished above Tottenham in the Premier League since the 2007/08 season – testament to the consistent improvement that Spurs have enjoyed over the last decade and a half. Matches against Spurs' east London neighbours, though, are always occasions to be relished.

★ HUGO LLORIS ★

144

Hugo Lloris has been Tottenham's goalkeeper since 2012, offering the team a generally safe last line of defence when it's needed. He started his career playing for his home town of Nice in the south of France, before heading in the right direction by joining Lyon and then making his home in north London. He has been Spurs' permanent captain since 2015.

In his debut season with Lyon, Lloris enjoyed 16 clean sheets and only conceded 27 goals in total, putting him firmly in the French league's team of the year.

He has also been a mainstay of the French national squad since 2008. They won the FIFA World Cup in 2018 (becoming runners-up in 2022), as well as the UEFA Nations League in 2020/21 after coming second in 2016.

As a lad, Lloris also excelled at tennis and was one of the top-ranked French players in his age group before hanging up his racket to concentrate on football.

Lloris has sometimes faced criticism for inconsistency and a lack of quality ball distribution, but to be fair to him – and goalies everywhere – it's a phenomenally difficult job when all eyes are on you. If a striker misses a sitter, it's generally greeted with a shrug and a smile, but when a goalie has a slip, the terraces can be very quick to criticise, which is often the last thing the goalie needs.

The reality is that Lloris has made a superb contribution to the club over the years, both as goalkeeper and captain. He is also a Knight in the French National Order of the Legion of Honour, which is a pretty cool thing to be.

EVERYONE LOVES A
★ CELEBRATION ★

Celebrating has always been a key part of football. Scoring is a difficult business, and sometimes you have to work really hard to get the ball into the back of the net, so it's not surprising that when goals come, they are joyous moments that bring fans and players together. Back in the day, when they were a thing, the back pages of the newspapers rarely showed photos of the goal being kicked – it was usually a group of players celebrating a goal and beaming at you as you tucked into your cornflakes.

Harry Kane's simple, iconic, kiss of his wedding ring seems to say as much about the man as a thousand interviews, while Jürgen Klinsmann diving to the ground to celebrate opening his Spurs account against Sheffield Wednesday lampooned his own reputation and endeared him to a generation of fans.

Obviously, football is a serious business, though, and the sport's authorities, conscious of their role as champions of morality in the 1970s, decided that they needed to clamp down hard on players when it looked like they were having too much fun. As a result, for the 1975/76 season, they attempted to ban exuberant celebrations after goals.

They proposed that any player who was deemed to have 'kissed and cuddled' another player on the field of play should be charged with bringing the game into disrepute. And it wasn't just the authorities in England: in the early 1980s, the world's governing bodies also tried to get in on the act by banning exuberant outbursts such as jumping on top of one another, kissing and embracing.

They might as well have tried to ban haircuts that weren't short back and sides.

The reality is that goal celebrations are fairly self-managing in the main. Back flips are very cool and all, but they are challenging from an insurance perspective, and players are conscious of how easy it is to get injured when jumping on top of each other. It's their livelihoods.

We can also thank VAR for calming things down a bit, because nothing's going to make you look sillier than scoring a goal, going into an extensive celebration routine and then realising halfway through that the voice from Stockley Park is whispering in the ref's ear and the goal is going to be scratched off. Opposition fans can be so understanding and are generally very quick to empathise. Save it for *Strictly*.

The ban on over-exuberant celebrations actually stood until 1996, although there is little evidence that anyone really tried to enforce it. Technically, there are still laws in place that are intended to discourage choreographed celebrations, though.

DEFINITION OF 'SPURSY':
CONSISTENTLY FAILING TO
LIVE UP TO EXPECTATIONS AND
TO FALL APART WITH VICTORY
IN ONE'S GRASP.

"THE GREAT FALLACY IS THAT THE GAME IS FIRST AND LAST ABOUT WINNING. IT IS NOTHING OF THE KIND. THE GAME IS ABOUT GLORY, IT IS ABOUT DOING THINGS IN STYLE AND WITH A FLOURISH, ABOUT GOING OUT AND BEATING THE OTHER LOT, NOT WAITING FOR THEM TO DIE OF BOREDOM."

Danny Blanchflower, defensive midfielder, explains the philosophy that made him a White Hart Lane legend.

"BILL EVENTUALLY BECAME MR TOTTENHAM HOTSPUR, AND PRODUCED SUCH A DAZZLING TEAM AT WHITE HART LANE THAT THEY WON THE DOUBLE AND PLAYED THE GAME IN A WAY THAT WAS AN OBJECT LESSON TO EVERYBODY."

Brian Clough

★ HARRY KANE ★

In a gilded era of football, where players live in mansions and arrive at training in supercars with matching designer tracksuits, Harry Kane is refreshingly humble. That's not to suggest that he doesn't live well, enjoy finely tailored suits or take his family to the best restaurants, it's just that he always seems to be fairly calm about it – which is very weird, because he has quietly carved out a phenomenal career for himself as captain of both Spurs and England.

While his team trophy cupboard might be relatively modest, he has won the Premier League Golden Boot three times, as well as the World Cup Golden Boot. In the 2020/21 Premier League season, he also won the Playmaker award for most assists, making him one of only three players to have both scored the most goals and provided the most assists in a single season (the others being Newcastle United's Andrew Cole in 1994/95 and Leeds United's Jimmy Floyd Hasslebaink in 1998/99). At the time of writing, he is also tied with Wayne Rooney for most prolific England goal scorer and has bagged the Premier League's third largest number of goals (after Wayne Rooney and Alan Shearer).

A few loan spells aside, and a brief initial period with the

Arsenal academy at the age of eight (they released him for lacking athleticism), local lad Kane has spent his entire career so far at Tottenham. The only real issue with him as a leader and a player is that he has made himself so good that most Spurs fans spend every transfer window with their hearts in their mouths doomscrolling the transfer deadline update websites as rumours link him with every other major club in the world.

No matter when he leaves, whether it's to retire or play somewhere else, there is little doubt that his heart will always be with Spurs.

THE
★ SPAGHETTI INCIDENT ★

One game between West Ham and Tottenham has a particular resonance. Let's go back to the final day of the 2005/06 season, where both Tottenham and Arsenal were in the running for next season's final Champions League place. The stakes were high, and perhaps if Tottenham had stuck to the steaks, history would have been different.

Tottenham were one point ahead of Arsenal and were playing West Ham at Upton Park. All they needed to do was match Arsenal's result at Wigan and they would clinch the coveted fourth spot and be off on the trail of European glory the next season. It would be nice to report that that's exactly what happened. Unfortunately ...

The Tottenham team were booked into a hotel near the home of the Hammers, and they got together for a meal the evening before the match. Ten players, including first team stalwarts Michael Carrick, Edgar Davids, Michael Dawson, Robbie Keane and Aaron Lennon, tucked into hearty plates of lasagne and spaghetti bolognese to make sure they had their strength up for the match ahead.

What was discovered later was that there was an outbreak of norovirus at the hotel, but what it meant in the short term was that three-quarters of the first team were up half the night and most of the following morning talking on the big white telephone. They were, frankly, in no state to play, let alone perform. West Ham beat a cobbled together and deeply beleaguered Spurs 2–1, Arsenal beat Wigan and sauntered off to Europe with a chuckle.

A full investigation by various authorities showed that there was no foul play involved in the outbreak, but, to this day, West Ham's fans throw toilet paper on to the pitch whenever they are playing Tottenham. Because they think they are funny.

It's impossible to say what would have happened if Spurs had won that match against West Ham. When you look at the names on the team sheet around that time, there were more than a handful of international players that could have helped Tottenham to shine on the biggest stage in football. It wasn't to be, though, so it's become another one to chalk up to experience.

It does not make Tottenham always the bridesmaid; it's simply another one of those things that will make victory taste all the sweeter when it eventually, inevitably, comes.

DIEGO MARADONA PULLED ON THE NUMBER 10 SHIRT FOR SPURS IN OSSIE ARDILES' TESTIMONIAL AGAINST INTER MILAN IN 1986. LINEKER WORE IT BETTER THOUGH.

Season	Player	Goals
2002/03	Teddy Sheringham/Robbie Keane	13
2003/04	Robbie Keane	16
2004/05	Jermain Defoe	22
2005/06	Robbie Keane	16
2006/07	Dimitar Berbatov	23
2007/08	Dimitar Berbatov/Robbie Keane	23
2008/09	Darren Bent	17
2009/10	Jermain Defoe	24
2010/11	Rafael van der Vaart	15
2011/12	Emmanuel Adebayor	18
2012/13	Gareth Bale	26
2013/14	Emmanuel Adebayor	14
2014/15	Harry Kane	31
2015/16	Harry Kane	28
2016/17	Harry Kane	35
2017/18	Harry Kane	41
2018/19	Harry Kane	24
2019/20	Harry Kane	24
2020/21	Harry Kane	33
2021/22	Harry Kane	27
2022/23	Harry Kane	32

Goals   0   5   10   15

TOTTENHAM'S LEADING GOAL SCORERS BY SEASON

★ ★

(PREMIER LEAGUE)

THE
★ TROPHY CABINET ★

Competition	Year
Premier League victories	Not yet
Football League Champions	1950/51, 1960/61
The FA Cup Winners	1900/01, 1920/21, 1960/61, 1961/62, 1966/67, 1980/81, 1981/82, 1990/91
Football League Cup Winners	1970/71, 1972/73, 1998/99, 2007/08
European Cup Winners' Cup Winners	1962/63
UEFA Cup Winners	1971/72, 1983/84
Football League Division Two Champions	1919/20, 1949/50
FA Charity Shield Winners	1921, 1951, 1961, 1962, 1967 (joint), 1981 (joint), 1991 (joint)